THE LITTLE YELLOW HOUSE

THE HUGH MACLENNAN POETRY SERIES

Editors: Allan Hepburn and Tracy Ware

Selection Committee: Mark Abley, Donald H. Akenson, Philip Cercone, and Joan Harcourt

TITLES IN THE SERIES

The Little Yellow House

HEATHER SIMENEY MacLEOD

McGill-Queen's University Press

Montreal & Kingston • London • Ithaca

© McGill-Queen's University Press 2012
ISBN 978-0-7735-4021-7

Legal deposit second quarter 2012
Bibliothèque nationale du Québec

Printed in Canada on acid-free paper that is 100% ancient forest free
(100% post-consumer recycled), processed chlorine free.

McGill-Queen's University Press acknowledges the support
of the Canada Council for the Arts for our publishing program.
We also acknowledge the financial support of the Government of
Canada through the Canada Book Fund for our publishing activities.

Library and Archives Canada Cataloguing in Publication

MacLeod, Heather,
    The little yellow house / Heather Simeney MacLeod.
    (The Hugh MacLennan poetry series)
    Poems.
    ISBN 978-0-7735-4021-7

    I. Title. II. Series: Hugh MacLennan poetry series

    PS8575.L4625L58 2012   811'.54   C2011-908452-X

This book was typeset by Interscript in 10.5/13 Sabon.

For Mazie Ann Beeds

CONTENTS

THE LITTLE YELLOW HOUSE

I remember. It is the summer of my crucifixion. I try so hard to be pure; I take two baths a day.

Richard Van Camp

These are the things that I know: so slender,
so small they slip in the spaces between us,
and they live in the gaps between everything else.
After your phone call, I sat on my bed
looking at the photograph of Edinburgh
at Christmas. Scott's monument is lit up
from the Ferris Wheel. After she died, I took
down all the art from the walls; I washed them
and smoothed down the holes from the nails.
And in the morning after – then I took the pieces
of what I knew and tried to make a whole.

A completeness of her: a painting, a photograph,
a silkscreen, something that would be all
of what she was – shy, melodramatic,
moody, and cranky. A lock of memory,
but there's nothing that can stand in place
of even the colour green except the colour green.
We must admit we, the living, collect the dead.
Fallen autumn leaves, crushed flowers between
the pages of books, photographs of moments
that can never be fully recovered or even
remembered, and we waste, we squander,

we misplace, we misremember, and we forget.

YOUR VOICE

It was your voice I heard long ago amid the crowds.
I heard it through caverns. I heard it in the long
forgetfulness of other lives when you and I lived
in the dark, blankness of short days
in damp caves and painted with charcoal,
from the fire, your first desires of fish and sea.
And when I saw you, two years ago, in brown

corduroy and a plaid, short-sleeved, cotton shirt
with small, delicate, egg-like buttons I *made myself*
look away. I remembered you from those other days
and thought in the back of myself, hidden from light
and knowing, *This is what they mean when they say
love at first sight,* that loving at first sight is a
    remembering.
Love at first sight is a kind of haunting, distant

lullaby, and when you spoke pieces of me
splintered, and a section of who I am ran to your side
and another fled from the room, and I stayed in my chair
pretending I didn't know you, pretending I did not
remember your voice, the sound of your timbre,
the clearing of your throat, the moan of your desire.
Pretending I didn't remember.

FISHERMAN ON THE BEACH

painted in the Hague: August, 1882

I feel Death moving over the leagues
of my sleep to take me to the summer
in Skidegate when I worked as a fisherman
on my uncle's boat. Death fetches me
over the kilometres of time. He pulls me
back falling underneath the blue folds
of the Pacific ocean. A blanket of memory
to cover me when Death first moved inside me,
and persuaded me to give up my struggling,
to take a deep breath and let life exhale
in one motion. Panic moved through me,
a dark baptism, salt water covered my lungs,
it was my brother who pulled me out
with Death still moving inside me. My brother
leaned over me and changed the liquid
pattern of my breath, and Death was caught
between water and air, caught in his slow
deliberation. Death is still inside me, still searching.

Was it this way for Vincent,
the way the bullet moved from the gun
into his chest, and Death went searching
with gradual consideration? And when Theo
came, he found Vincent sitting up in bed;
the bullet still moving inside him,
like a hook in a fish, looking for a way out.

ON THE REVOLUTIONS OF THE CELESTIAL ORBS

Scripture teaches us how to go to Heaven, not how the heavens go. – Galileo

One of the first things you told me, *I lived on Copernicus
    Street*
in the Hague, and asked if I knew who Copernicus was,
    and I did.

Nicolaus Copernicus was born in 1473 and died in 1543.
He published *Revolutionibus Orbium Coelestium* the
same year he died and dedicated it to Pope Paul III.
Copernicus was the founder of the heliocentric plane-
tary theory – the theory of a sun-centred solar system
as opposed to an earth-centred solar system – he said,
mathematically, *We are not the centre of the universe.*

I remember, you told me living on Copernicus Street
reminded you, you were not the centre of things.
You used the word, *things* because you didn't want to say
her name, *Hedda*. You didn't want to say, *How strange
to find myself on Copernicus Street in the Hague
learning how we revolve around one another, and then
suddenly how we don't – just as if an astronomer arrived
at my doorstep to tell me how sometimes it happens,
I am loved and then I am not loved. How I am the centre –
all celestial bodies rotating around me – and then
I am not the centre, and her body rotates around
    someone else.*

I wanted to talk of synchronicity; Carl Jung's theory
of meaningful coincidence because while you lived
in the Hague thinking of the name Copernicus – I lived
in Seattle, in the Central District, and woke three times
in the early mornings saying out loud, *Copernicus.*
I looked the name up because I thought it came
from a Shakespeare play, or from some other piece
of literature. I thought it came to me like serendipity,
like synchronicity, and I thought it arrived with meaning.
Instead I found only a handful of references on the Internet
to a holy man. He published a book, dedicated to the pope,
the year he died, and it was eventually placed
on the Catholic's forbidden book list.

Many generations from now a young girl will read
a book by Stephen King. The book is about a werewolf,
and the girl will have many sleepless nights and many
nightmares. And, so, her brother will take her to a silversmith,
and using her Saint Margaret's medallion and the chain
it hangs on forge a silver bullet. The only way
to slay a werewolf. The Saint Margaret's medallion
will be old and thick with sentimental value. The girl
will know the story of Saint Margaret.

Saint Margaret of Antioch was popular in the Middle
Ages. Probably most popular because she met the devil
in the form of a dragon, and when he swallowed her, the
cross she wore so irritated him, he was forced to dis-
gorge her. She's usually depicted with a dragon under
her feet and is commonly known as Saint Margaret the
Dragonslayer. Hers, along with Saint Michael and Saint
Catherine, was one of the voices heard by Joan of Arc.

The girl will tell her brother, on the way to the
   silversmith,
Saint Margaret is one of the saints who came to Joan of
   Arc.
The girl's imagination is like a piece of textured cloth,
and she will tell her brother, *Saint Margaret is the one.*
She's the one who whispered to Joan of Arc, "Now.
Attack.
Now.
Don't fall back,
don't give up."
Maybe, the girl says to her brother as he glances over to
   her,
his hands gripping the steering wheel just a little tighter,
Saint Margaret was the one who guided Joan against the
   English.
The one who said, "Raise your sword against them.
Now."
Whose voice do you think she heard in the fire?

Her brother thinks, *The bullet*
will make a better medallion than Saint Margaret.

My first middle name, the one given me by my mother
and not given by the cult I found myself in when I was
in my twenties, was Joan. Once, while going through
your wallet, I found your landed immigrant certificate
and asked how you pronounced your middle name
which was written the same as my first middle name,
   Joan.
You said, *Johann. It's a boy's name, but not here.*
I was going to tell you, how it was once my middle name

as well, but then you said, *It's not my middle name now.*
Now I go by John. And I thought how odd, we both
had the same first middle name and renamed ourselves.
You seemed, to me, so utilitarian, I never asked you
of synchronicity. The closest I got to it was when I
asked you about choices and destiny, and you told me
that you shouldn't have taken me to see *Run Lola Run.*

❧

A bullet finds its life when it's fired from the gun;
     perhaps,
the same way the gun finds its life only once the trigger
is pulled, and then it falls still again, lifeless.

The girl wore the bullet, which in its first life was a
     medallion
of a saint, around her neck. It hung on a piece of leather
and rested against her heart. She gave the bullet
away to a young boy who wore a brown velour shirt
in her tenth grade Algebra class. Because she loved him.
Loved him with all of her length, with the fullness
of her fifteen years. She wanted to please him and, so,
she gave him the item, which she loved the best.
He wore it for a little while, then threw it
into his fishing tackle box and forgot about it.

❧

I have mapped our lives from before we knew one
     another.
The cities we were in at the same time; the movie houses
we both sat in, watching the same movies, the same days.
I'd like to go back to the Northills Cinema on Boxing Day,
and find you sitting four rows in front of me and to the left

watching the second matinee of *Titanic*. I want to tell you
not about love, not about the way your fist pierced
my heart, not about the way you pulled your fist out,
and plunged it in again, deeper. I want to tell you
about synchronicity. I want to ask you,
Do you believe in meaningful coincidence?

Joan of Arc found a sword in a field; she believed God
placed it there guiding her toward her destiny. It's a
    meaningful
coincidence that Joan of Arc found a sword in a field,
but only meaningful when we look back.
At the time she found the sword, it didn't mean,
really, anything. Joan's sword in the field resembles the
    measure
of the moment when I went to the Northills Cinema
on Boxing Day, to the second matinee
of *Titanic*. This event only gained meaning when I
    placed you
in it. That we were so close and didn't know one another.
I hadn't fallen in love with you. You were just another
    person
sitting in the cinema watching a movie. My heart
was without the wounds you plunged into it.
There was no drama living between us. There were only
red seats, cement floor, a wide screen, darkened room,
with two exit signs glowing like a warning,
guideposts to the direction I should have taken
with you, but didn't.

Really, she thinks much later, *it was as if the gun
found the bullet on its own.* She doesn't recall going

through the fishing tackle box, and even if she had,
couldn't have been looking for a bullet, and certainly
not that particular bullet which was made to kill
something unholy. It was all fitting in the end.
When people say, *Honey, don't worry, it all works out
in the end,* they're right. Somehow, in the end, it all
fit together. Pieces falling into slots, which she
couldn't have imagined. *God weaves a tapestry,*
she told her lawyer, and he sighed heavily
and typed some notes on his laptop.

I want to ask you, which is the reason I do not call,
*How can you allow someone else's body to rotate
     around your own?*
How does it happen? How does it happen that I am loved,
and then I am not loved? How I was once your centre,
and you mine. You, the one, a celestial body I rotated
around, and now you move, circle around someone else.
I want to ask you, as if I am still a child standing
in a field of blue with an open pink heart,
Why don't you love me?

Her brother brings her the old Stephen King novel.
He asks if she's sure before he brings it,
worries it will give her nightmares as it did before.
She reads it carefully. She finds hidden meaning
in the words, and when she can't find any meaning
she removes words with a black felt and begins
to make up messages. She doesn't think
she's made them up. Everything has value,
everything has meaning. It simply needs to be uncovered.

She found a bullet in a fishing tackle box,
but it was the gun that went searching for it.
The gun needed the bullet not her.
Joan of Arc found a sword in a field.
Destiny is announced in the mildest of a breeze.
Saint Margaret was beheaded in prison,
and Joan of Arc burned at the stake as a heretic.
Now and then she tries to explain the life of the bullet.
How it slipped into the gun on its own,
and how it slipped out of the gun just as easily.
How it whispered, *No celestial body
rotates around me.* She felt sorry for the bullet
as it whispered through the air. How it flew
through his brown velour shirt, how it found
(and this was really a miracle because she'd never
fired a gun before) his heart. How it stopped there.
She tells the judge, *The bullet was silent then.
It wasn't whispering Saint Margaret's instructions
to Saint Joan and it wasn't muttering, "Copernicus,"
over and over again. It's as if that's where it always
wanted to be. The bullet was destined to rest
in his heart. It longed to get there.*

❧

A bullet comes into its life once fired from the gun.
There is a bullet moving through a blue field;
it's searching for a pink heart.
Saint Margaret through the air whistling, *Copernicus,*
and landing; pushing through the bone to the vital organ
where before it rests, it says, *Attack. Now. Don't give up.
Don't
give
up.*

CHURCH AT AUVERS-SUR-OISE

painted in Auvers-sur-Oise: June, 1890

The church is alive, as alive as Gauguin's chair.
That's the thing with *things* – they speak
and breathe and move among and between us.
When Vincent left the south of France
he was alone. He moved and breathed
among strangers, and he died not far
from the seething church. It undulates
as if it is about to embark upon
a great exhalation. It holds its breath

in a country I cannot know. In the world
of my upbringing churches are often made
from planks of wood; they live alone
in fields that no longer mark crossroads.
Abandoned in unkempt meadows
in city streets, abandoned in unkempt
meadows of village roads, abandoned
in unkempt meadows and acres broken
by cattle and dried up river beds,

the churches in my country barely breathe.

In the beginning because that is what they call it:
the beginning as if nothing came before the light,
as if nothing came before Adam and Eve.
Wasn't I here then? Certainly, I remember

the seraph the one that guards the tree
of wisdom, the one that guards the fruit
with a thin-layered silver sword.
Aren't his wings made of muscle and tendon?

Isn't his sword real, doesn't his blade cut
through the air? Shouldn't Eve be celebrated?
Her curiosity was as layered as the seraph's blade.
I pulled her toward the tree. I enticed her.

It was easily done. Adam stood mute as if silence
could be mistaken for disagreement.
She reached up and plucked that fruit,
which wasn't even yet fully ripe.

And she took it into her mouth, and not
because she longed for wisdom or knowledge
for she couldn't, yet, understand either,
but rather her curiosity drove her to bite

through the skin, to taste the bitter fruit.
Punishment arrived so swiftly,
but I believe even now, as I did then,
that He wanted us to know the fruit.

Didn't He want us to eat our way through
to the knowing; to eat our way past wisdom
into innocence? Wasn't His intention
with the order to avoid the eating of that fruit failure?

Didn't He want one of them, Adam or Eve, to succumb?
Didn't He make me with the trickster's intentions?
Didn't He make me to dwell in mischievous delight?
Wasn't His intention as he formed me

from the red dirt at Adam's feet
for me to entice Eve to the first taste of sin,
the first taste of separation. Eve's gift
is the intense longing, the bitter desire to know

God as we once did, the three of us,
in that quiet space. I am all but forgotten
after the story is told. I am left to the punishment
of eating dust, crawling through grass,

but everything is clearer here. I followed
Adam's first step from the garden and fell
into the hollow shape of his heel,
but I am unlike any other animal, which moves

through the world, for I lived in Eden
and I delivered the fruit of knowledge
and I circled the tree of wisdom
and I saw the seraph's blade move through the air.

WHEN ERIN FOUGHT BESIDE
JOAN OF ARC

she knew the taste of a Catholic God inside her mouth,
and Joan's lost chains still ring and grind in Erin's dreams.

She's forgotten how many soldiers her sword took down,
and she's forgotten the blood-soaked banner, which waved

above her head. She's forgotten the saints which lived
so tightly within her, she once swore she heard the voice

of Saint Margaret speaking through the mouth of Joan.
She's forgotten how Joan turned the English army

back with nothing but the sound of her voice.
Once Joan taught Erin everything she believed

she'd ever need to know about God.
When Erin fought at the side of Joan of Arc she believed;

she rode and raised her sword beside the perfect weapon
of God held in the flawed body of humanity. Erin blames

the Catholic God, the one, which sent Joan messages
for the English fire that ripped at Joan, but maybe

Saint Margaret was there in the flames still whispering
in Saint Joan's ears? When Saint Joan's memory

travels towards Erin, it's in the feel of a blade,
the crack of wood in a fire, a banner waving

white and blue in a parade,
the taste of red wine in her mouth.

In the fields of Metchosin,
her mouth moistened, glistened,
slightly red, a wooden basket
almost filled, lying on the ground,
and her fingers over everything
he would eat. He concealed a wedge
of apple amid blackberries for the pie;
and she took, maybe without meaning,
maybe by misfortune, his touch from

the apple, his hollowed hand, the other
peeling, his thumb shifted slow steps
across crimson apple skin. She took
the taste of him, and he placed a portion
of apple in the blackberry pie because
he wanted the unexpected, wanted her
to feel foreign in her mouth, to feel
the unfamiliar skipping across her tongue,
hiding between her teeth. He needed her

to know he'd take God away from her,
and she couldn't blame anyone
because he'd warned her with a piece
of apple, warned her, a wounded boy
in the fields, if he couldn't hear God
then neither would she; he took the sound of
Christ in his hand and peeled the voice
of God away from her, the hollowed
shape of his fist all she could see.

THE POTATO EATERS

painted in Nuenen: April, 1885

It came to me like a young boy,
as if I knew where it stood,
with hair the colour of flax
lying, ready to be spun,
in my grandmother's hands.
It came to me in the morning,
but I put it aside and rode
my bicycle through McArthur Park
and turned Van Gogh's painting
of the potato eaters over
in my mind, the shape of needing.
I comfort myself with stolen objects –
it's what the poor have left
when they've put aside things
like honour and integrity.
When they've put on the coat of distress.
It came back, circled toward me
like a magpie in the prairie fields
of grain and earth and sky;
it came on dark wings: the difference
between wanting and needing.
The difference like a young boy, flaxen haired
in the meadows, barefoot and thin.

When he comes to bed it's the smell of cheap,
hotel soap; or sometimes it's ivory slick and slippery
over his skin; other times it's pink-grapefruit
from the Body Shop, which has pushed its way
behind his ears and the back of his neck.
She recognizes raspberry nectar and lemon zinger
purchased from the round barrels of London Drugs.
When he leaves her in the mornings he smells
of the only soap she buys; its clean cinnamon
scent over his skin, and when he comes home,
she can trace his travels by aroma.
She imagines the women he covers by the
smell their soap leaves behind on his skin.

THEN SHE'D KNOW

What if she went – to that museum, gallery,
and the coffee-house which host
poetry and spoken-word open mics –
and found them for him? Saved
him the trouble of looking. Saved herself
the trouble of waiting up. What then?
She knows who would satisfy him.
The way he looks at the photographer

with short, dusty blonde hair, which is cropped
close to her scalp like a stunted field of barley,
and her eyes a meadow of rain-beaten
alfalfa. And she'd be behind the Japanese screen,
unblinking, her breath coming from her chest
in short, shallow gasps, which he'd mistake
for desire. Sunday morning she could bring him
the painter from Zimbabwe – her skin is mocha,

her hair curled double-knots of black silk –
and over brunch he'd smile, and tell her
how the woman tasted of coffee. He could
remark upon the succulent lather of her sweat,
still a memory on his tongue.
Then she would know whose flesh his hands
move over. Whose body he enters, then she'd know.
She wouldn't be left waiting, she'd be busy bathing

their seasoned skin, washing their hair of silk mesh,
and laying them on the bed, which she'd be sure
smelled of orange blossoms. She'd keep dried lotus
petals on the windowsill and Marianne Faithfull
on the stereo. All these things she'd do for him,
bending herself like a fine willow reed. Leaving
herself empty as a vessel, empty as a saint,
empty as a stalk of bamboo.

TOOK HER AND CRADLED HER
IN HIS ARMS

Electra at the Tomb of Agamemnon, Frederic Leighton, 1869

When he came home, tired from the journey,
he was remembering how he had carried her
cradled in his arms, the night of their wedding.
How he had lifted her, she was so slight,
and held her as if she was not only wife,
but child and mother. How he held her,
cradled, and murmured soft words against
her upswept hair. She shook in his arms,
and he had wondered for many years
if she had shaken due to fear or desire,
and as he walked up the stone steps to his home
decided tonight he would finally ask her,
and how he hoped the answer would be, *desire*.

When he walked down the corridor toward her chamber
she stepped out from the darkness,
it had been so long since he had set his eyes upon her
and her hair was long and loose and her feet were bare,
and she said his name, and he was smiling
when he received the first blow and his desire fell
around him bright red ribbons of blood.

He wanted to tell her how he had come home
to carry her back to him, he had come home
to cradle her in his arms.

THE BEDROOM IN THE YELLOW HOUSE,
AN INTERIOR WITHOUT ANYTHING:
IN THREE PARTS

The Bedroom, 1888, Van Gogh Museum
Van Gogh's Bedroom in Arles, 1889, Musée d'Orsay
The Bedroom, 1889, The Art Institute of Chicago

PART I

They arrived in Amsterdam just before Christmas.
It seemed mild after the snow-covered streets
of London. She felt like they were on a great adventure,
and ripped from the kitchen wall of the hostel,
in Amsterdam, a square sticker that said:
we travel to be lost. At the time it seemed profound,
but now she thinks it sounds lonely. The first day she
    wanted

to buy pottery dishes decorated with thick dragonflies
from Portugal, but never had enough money.
She's kept the ticket from the Van Gogh Museum.
She remembers the museum like she remembers
    Amsterdam:
it was small and filled with light. Van Gogh believed
that objects, *things,* take on their owner's personality
like a room when emptied of its occupant.

PART II

She went to the old train station the second morning.
Her calves were still sore from climbing the stairs
of the Eiffel Tower the night before. She was alone,
but taken with a beautiful man she'd met
on Lothian Road in Edinburgh. She spent most
of the morning sitting beside François Pompon's
Polar Bear. Pompon concentrated on the essence

of the bear, but for her, so far from home, it seemed
the essence of Canada. She, who once drunkenly
had claimed to love the space between places,
felt a desire to be rooted, and the bus tickets,
train tickets, and plane tickets zipped into the side
of her bag made her feel a mixture of loneliness
and longing. When she found Van Gogh's bedroom

from the little yellow house, it drained her of everything
but a need to see home. That rise of the arctic,
on the plane, after Greenland when the land
of her country rolls itself out like an ocean,
and she was taken with the memory of him,
and she whispered his name over the tundra,
and she whispered his name over the prairies,

and she whispered his name into the Pacific Ocean,
and his name was just a sigh in Canada.

PART III

It's the last of the three, the third painting,
in Chicago that she likes the best. The floor is solid
and green; the light is thicker coming in through
the opened window to the bedroom in the little
yellow house. Van Gogh described it as
"an interior without anything," but maybe
it is his absence that he regrets.

And these are the last of the words
he writes down for her, and these are the first
of the words he writes down for himself.
And he writes them on a Starbucks napkin
with a blue ball-point pen, and admires her

fingernails which she's gone and painted pink,
and she blots her lipstick on his napkin.
She leaves pink impressions across the surface,
and he writes her name over and over again.
Then he says out loud, *Enough*. He takes her

lipstick and draws a line across the napkin.
Maybe he needs some sort of physical proof
that he's said, *Enough*. But she ignores him,
and shakes her index finger in his face.
I watch her shouting at him all the way to the car,

and his hands beat back at the air. And I'm
playing with a long strand of my hair,
biting at my lower lip, and he comes back in,
and she goes into the washroom crying.
And I take out, from the front pocket of my

blue jeans *Paradise Plum* lipstick, and I say
to the man, *Haven't you had enough?*
And she comes out of the bathroom,
and he sees beautiful sadness when she asks him,
Are you mad at me? And I recognize him

– just like one of the little boys
from kindergarten. He's just like Michael
who had blond hair and gentle eyes, or maybe
like David who loved me *crazy* when I was eight.
And I watch as he reaches out to touch her, and I know

how he hasn't had enough – not even close to *enough*.
I pick up the napkin after they've left,
and see them walking hand-in-hand to their car.
She's kissing and kissing him, and I imagine my lipstick
Paradise Plum all over both of them,

it's sweet and pungent and irresistible.
And she's all fairy-tales and lipstick and painted nails
and loose-fitting, button-fly, faded denim, 501, Levi's,
and he can take and take and keep on taking because
he has *no* idea what love looks like. And I look down

at the stream of words that he's left behind
on the Starbucks paper napkin and the first word is,
    I,
and the last word is,
    her.

FOREIGN EUCHARIST

His past trails behind him on the trains
and in the cracks of cobbled walkways.
It follows him into the transepts
of Romanesque basilicas. It leaves

no room for foreign languages,
but slight space for convenient phrases.
Empty, small words and sayings
sit alive on his tongue. He spends

too much time walking across
strange city streets, standing in trams
and tubes, swaying on ferries.
He is unguided. He slips out

from under his own footsteps.
Wakes in the middle of the night,
thick cream from foreign tins
covering his arches and soles.

He slips his feet between starched
cotton sheets; each callous dreams
in German. His past follows him
as if he built it from brick and stone,

from stained glass, used flying buttresses,
and vaulted ceilings. He becomes
a Gothic cathedral that storms through
his dreams. Sleeping, he finds a gilded Christ

becoming a globe opening on his palm.
He can't take him up. He can't ask for more.

He loves her like a small demon in the blood.
He loves her before and he loves her during,
and he loves her through their travels in Europe,
and even though he shouldn't, he loves her after.
If he wasn't in his forties, I'd shrug and tell him
how it happens. How it happens that so many
head off with their backpacks and their passports,
and their boyfriends or girlfriends,

and come back broke and single, but happy,
or something sort of resembling happy.
Or at least they come back with experience and souvenirs,
but that's not the thing you can tell someone
when they love someone they shouldn't
like a small demon in their blood.
And just before Hope he starts talking, and it's a blur
of beds, breakfasts, hotels, hostels, trains, trams,

tubes, towns, cities, churches, cathedrals,
sights, sounds, mosques, mementoes, and despair.
But maybe he can get her back, what do I think?
Wha'do I think? I pull into the Dairy Queen at Hope,
park illegally and we eat in the car. Well, wha'do I think?
Maybe she'll come find him, maybe he'll be heading
out into the pasture one morning and she'll be there.
Wha'do I think? It's different when you're on a boat

heading from Patros to Venice. He's quiet.
Stares out the window. What's that,
that Ed always says about his ex-wife Roxanne?
Do I remember? How's Ed, by the way? Is he still
ranching out Meadow Lake way, or is he back in the
    bush
falling? Beachcombing in Rivers Inlet, I tell him.
Watsit he usdta say? His accent keeps shifting between
city and country. Do I remember, how Ed'd say

Roxanne left him 'cause she hadda
find some meat for her weasel. He's not waiting.
He's not waiting for her. No, not him he's nobody's
    chump.
He's got me a pretty little glass pendant from Milan,
and a key chain from Athens; did I get his postcards?
Do I think she'll come back? Have I heard from her?
He loves her, don't I know, how he loves her?
He luvs'r like a fuken demon in'nis blood.

He walked the Bridge of Sighs, placed one foot
right before the other from palace to prison,
then back again. It felt like when he turned ten,
and saw the curve of his life spiral ahead of him
like a ball on a piece of string. He fed pigeons
in the square outside the east transept
of Saint Mark's Basilica. They fluttered around
him, rested on his shoulders, made him more

than a middle-aged man with torn-up Wranglers
and calloused hands, turned him into beloved
    architecture
– adored and admired by Italian pigeons everywhere.
He tried to photograph every winged-lion he saw
until he was so exhausted he felt them
in his hands, his feet, and his chest. And Saint Mark
roared through his dreams and whimpered
into the dark sleep of his loneliness. He reined

in disappointment up and down the Grand Canal
for all the gondolas tied up at the docks.
Leaving, he sat in the cold winter train station
with an American who offered him red wine
from the bottle, and who shared English with him
like it was a pomegranate resting on a porcelain plate,
the pleasant sound of, *hello, how are you?*

STILL LIFE:
BOTTLE, LEMONS AND ORANGES

painted in Arles: May, 1888

In the train station, I see him and he's with her.
I imagine a cheap green bottle of red wine
in his Salvation-Army-winter-coat pocket
and know this is how he will say, *Good-bye.*
Because this is how he thinks it's done,
abandonment, but he doesn't finish
the word and instead stops with, *abandon.*
And *o*, but it tastes so sweet in his mouth,
for a moment he doesn't want to share it,
not even with her, and when he finally
pushes it along his molars, past his chipped
front tooth, he feels practically drunk, giddy
with the release, with the cutting of the ropes.
Abandon, he says and smiles and she smiles back.
I see them sit together, the bottle of wine makes
a rough clatter against the benches which line up
like pews, and make me feel as if I should bend
myself, one heavy knee to another, and offer
up acts of contrition, forgiveness. And I hear him
from several benches up telling her *surrender*
is another word for abandon. He makes it sound
so good, I could lift it up like fruit, peel it back,
one thick strip after another and bite in, careless.
Surrender to the taste of abandon, to the taste of
    good-bye.

THE CITY OF RABBITS

A Young Hare, Albrecht Dürer, 1502

Before she came here, to the city of rabbits, she lived
in a city that smelled of toast. Walking
down Morningside Road, she'd smell bread.
The thick coat of yeast moving from Haymarket
to Marchmont over the graveyard to Clerk Street

past the Morrisons, Waitroses, and Tescos,
and the smell of toast followed her through the life
she lived when she lived in Scotland. And here,
everywhere she goes Dürer looks back at her with
    longing
and regret. Everywhere she goes the rabbits greet her

in the back alleys, in streets, across bridges,
in the river valley, in parking lots, and they fill her
up with all their yearning and remorse.
They're not floppy-eared bunnies, or soft-coated rabbits
nibbling their way through the campus in Victoria.

These are Dürer's rabbits, lean and wild.
A long time ago and in a land that seems far away,
she lived in a world filled with sagebrush and sunshine.
Before the rain in the city of toast, she lived in the
    semi-arid
blush of silt bluffs and prickly pear cacti. But here she is,

in the league of snow and ice. Her freckles have faded
into milk, and the rabbits follow her through Strathcona
and into the tree-lined streets of Garneau. They eat the
    trail
she leaves behind of greens and carrots. And Dürer's
    rabbits
enunciate loneliness in their wild spark and restless
    stretch.

she stepped from the garden into Cape Breton.
A wee place like New Waterford,
and she miraculously wore Levi's,
Doc Marten boots, and a black wool sweater
decorated with silver, square studs along the collar.

She liked the smell of the seawater in the air,
and found there was a faded lilt
to her speech, and she couldn't stop smiling.
She reached into her pocket and pulled out
a hand-rolled cigarette, and she lit up.

She breathed in deeply, saltwater in the air,
and exhaled pale, blue, Player's Light
extra mild, cigarette smoke
into the early morning breeze.
It feels good, she said, but Adam wasn't listening.

He couldn't figure out how to tie up his boots,
and he was coughing, and his eyes were watering,
and he couldn't tell if it was from the seawater,
thick smell of it in the air,
or the pale, blue cigarette smoke

Eve had exhaled directly into his up-turned face.
He stood up awkwardly, having tied the laces
up only on one boot. And he was thinking how he'd
    have to,
now, just make the best of it. Thinking how,
now, everything was closed to him, and he was thinking
    how,

now, everything would be so much harder.
Then he stumbled on a stray lace from his boot.
Eve couldn't stop smiling, and she bent and tied
his boot up for him and tossed her cigarette
on the ground and stepped on it. She couldn't wait

to tell Adam how she had realized that,
now, everything was open for them.
Couldn't wait to tell him how everything,
now, would be easier and marveling how,
now, they could really make the best of it.

The angels in the morning, the city still sleeping,
sun just rising, smell of smoke from the evening's
festivities still lingering in the air, lamb's blood
lulling through the streets, a baby weeping

several houses down, the sound of an old man
with his donkey walking across the flagstone
city streets of Sodom. *Don't turn back.*
Irit's back straight at the end of the bed

as the angels, in the morning, began bidding Lot
to rise and to take her and their two daughters,
the two in the house with them, and flee Sodom
for the wrath of God in the form of thousands

of angels hung above the city. *Don't turn back.*
Irit heard the angels their voices rising Lot
from his sleep noted how they did not turn
to address her, noted how they seemed

so much like her, so much like ordinary men,
the thick belly of the one, soft stubble
of a beard of another. *Don't look back.*
She sat at the edge of the bed her belongings

neatly packed, waiting. Lot stumbled out of bed
and she couldn't help herself she hissed toward him,
How could you sleep? He said nothing,
didn't even help her carry the bags, didn't mention

the two eldest of their daughters sleeping
in the city, and how soft their sleeping, how thick
their thinking they would never know God's fire.
Don't turn back. Lot stumbling about, a fool

and she wondered if her husband, like a half-baked
village idiot, wouldn't offer up her virgin daughters
for the pleasure of these angels from God yet again.
Don't look back. She thought how like a lamb

her husband was and thought how easily her blade
would slide over his throat, the water of his blood
falling to the ground and how she could offer
Lot the lamb to God as a sacrifice. *Don't turn back,*

but she did for her desire was to see
her eldest daughters following along behind
– their thick, black hair waving through the smoke
of sulfur and brimstone. Look back to behold them

rising from the ashes of God's fist and turn back
to see them wearing the dark, brown tunics
she'd made, the soft cotton sliding over their flesh.
Look back for even though she knew they would not

be coming she wanted to know what they knew.
She would follow them, and she was punished
because she disobeyed. But as she felt herself
fall still, an angel came to her with a soft voice,

and she knew, as the angel wept over her body
crystallizing her form with tears into salt, that
God had pity for her. And God had love for her,
and God understood why she had to look back.

REBECCA

I dreamed the knife for years,
dreamed the knife, felt it against
my throat, my body bound.
I dreamed the ram, the knife lifted,

knots cut away, blood running
down the altar, thick coat of it
against the stones. I dreamed.
I dreamed the knife. When I went

to fetch the water from the well
and bent down low to allow Isaac
to drink from the full vessel
at my head I recognized him

from the dream, from when I dreamed
the knife. The fullness of who I was
and who I am always like the filled
water jug at my head, *I live in my head,*

in my dreams for I dreamed the knife.
The rest of me empty, the rest of me
barren for I knew, for I dreamed
because I dreamed the knife.

I asked Hagar to return, to come back
to us with Ishmael as if I could undo
what had been done as if I could make
retribution for another woman's sins.

I sent for Ishmael, bid him to come to me
in my tent and wanted him with body,
with all my barrenness suddenly a blessing,
wanted him to take everything away from me,

to strip me bare, to force me down,
but a slight drizzle came, and he heard God in it,
and fled. Isaac came as if God sent him pounding
down with the rain and, so, my barrenness left.

Me, a full vessel and finally my curse had come
two-fold for my wickedness. Me, I was meant
to carry the jug, I was meant to offer the water,
I was not meant to be the vessel for I was the one,

it was me, I dreamed the knife. In the end,
of course, it was only in the end that I could see
it clearly. In my dreams the ram turned into Esau,
and I knew how it was I hadn't dreamed the knife

over Isaac with Abraham holding the blade,
but rather I held the knife over Esau
and it was me, I was the one, to sacrifice a son.
I should have stayed empty, should have

remained unmarked, my blood should never
have been allowed to slip down my thighs,
loss of my purity, I should have remained singular.
How sad it is to have dreamed the knife,

the way I tied Esau with ropes he couldn't see,
the way I let his blood fall, the way I turned
from the ram. The way I dreamed the knife.
The way I fulfilled my destiny against my own desires.

SHE REMEMBERS

After Jesus died, there was a young girl
waiting on the steps of a house on a hill
overlooking Jerusalem. In the house, a man
says he'll leave, now, for Ephesus;
he's going to write it all down; he's
going to make it real, make it matter.

He mentions John's death, and the young
woman dancing with his head on a tray;
and from the house they murmur suffering.
And the girl on the steps of a house on a hill
overlooking Jerusalem remembers Herod
calling John – the camel clothed, the locust

eating, the dung-heap John the Baptist.
Peter comes to the door with a glass
of sweet wine, and the girl smiles
at Peter trying to take away his shame.
Mary comes up the steps tells Peter
they've taken his body, and Mary leads

a few of them to the tomb, but the girl
stays at the steps of the house on the hill
overlooking Jerusalem. Years later she's filled
with regret. Lives later she sits in denim and cotton
t-shirts and cowboy boots thinking
of the God and not the man.

Thinks of Jesus with His arms outstretched
in supplication, glowing like chunks of amber,
but when she's sleeping she remembers
the man before the lashing,
before the crown of thorns, no sacred heart
outside his chest, and she remembers

the man stumbling in the streets of Jerusalem,
the smell of holly glutinous and thick,
and nothing in the air, but birds
and all their singing. And she sees herself
in plain fabric, barefoot, on stone steps
of a house on a hill overlooking a town.

God calls her, her hair a field of sunflowers
off Highway 1 through Saskatchewan.
God calls her forward out of the meadows
of Scotch Broom, out of the car with three
empty bottles of Pale Ale rolling back and forth.
God calls her out of Bear Canyon, out from the first

layer of Alberta snow, out from the rolling hills
of the Peace River Valley. God calls her.
She sees angels everywhere. She looks out
the car window driving north from Lemon Creek
and sees an angel with its face pressed up against
the window to her own. When she pulls the car

over at the steep bank of Goat River she sees
an angel filled with loneliness, and imagines it slips
inside her pale, blue skin. She feels the angel burrow
its way beneath her ribs. And her ribs are fully exposed
each segment easily drawn in her flesh.
She is a white martyr standing before God

with an angel underneath her skin.
Her body is a temple of starving contrition,
an offering of flesh as thin as a Catholic wafer.
This is how she wants to give herself away,
hidden behind a façade of transubstantiation.
God calls her, her eyes like lapis at the bottom

of mountain creek-beds. She thinks it's God
calling her forward with a flashlight
and an angel filled with loneliness. She thinks
God calls her into the Sun Kee Orchard
to find the young Québécois sleeping in his tent.
She hears God calling her through the bent streets

of Managua where she kneels at the toe
of Sandino's boot, and watches an angel grip
itself to her from the shadow of Sandino's
submachine gun. God calls her, her hair an orchard
filled with yellow apples. God calls her forward,
but she's lost in the pastures of the Kootenays picking
    cherries.

She names her perversion redemption; she names
her perversion hunger; she names her perversion
love, and meets men with ocher dreadlocks and thick
accents and cherry-stained hands, calling them
angel. God calls her, her eyes like cobalt
lake water under the winter snow.

WHEAT FIELD WITH CROWS

painted in Auvers-sur-Oise, July, 1890

I bring you a loaf of fresh sourdough,
and twist it, hot in my hands,
into separate halves.
Sheep woke us in the middle of the night,
with the moon slipping behind
the farmer's old stone fence, and you softly
moving against my back then over me. I could
hardly see your face, and ran my hands over
your features to feel the look of your pleasure.

I dreamed Ireland removed and Canada
re-built around me, so when I lifted the flap
of the tent in the morning I found Saskatchewan,
a wheat field with crows.

And you said, *Take. Eat. This is my body,*
and passed me a piece of sourdough
covered with peanut-butter, thick like lava.
I watched the peanut-butter melt into the bread,
bit into it finally, steam rolled out of my mouth,
you kissed me with your pleasure to be in the damp,
rolling hills outside of Dublin. The pleasure to be woken
in the night by a farmer's sheep, and to lie next
to a woman you think you love. And me,
desperate to feel wheat in my hands, snow
underneath my feet, crows in my eyes.

AN IMPOSSIBLE NOTION

I expected every day to be new
to be unlike any other day
or moment that came before or after.
It took me a long time to know,
to understand what it means: constant.
And I railed against
such a blasphemy, such an impossible
notion for many, long, heavy,
downtrodden, beaten days until I saw
what it means: the same.
Then I chose a pattern.
Coloured inside the lines.
Went to work.
Went to work on time.

Paid my bills.
Fell in love. Got married.
Wore down a path in the world
and celebrated my path I called: the same.
Cooked and cleaned
and cooked and cleaned some more.
Fought and argued
and fought and argued some more.
And the sun shines,
and then it shines some more.
And regret no longer filled with lamentation,
but instead with a sense of grace.
Love something that lived past passion,
and cut and sliced its way into affection.

And loss came, and it carried with it grief,
and they travelled together along the same path.
And when grief held me it told me,
I would never be *the same*.
I expected every day to be the same
to be like every other day
or moment that came before or after.
It took me a long time to know,
to understand what it means: random.
And I railed against
such a blasphemy, such an impossible
notion for many, long, heavy,
downtrodden, beaten days until I saw
what it means: impulsive.

THE SMALL BURIALS

She was born in winter,
stretched season of disappearing.
The vanishing of failures,
settled into snow.
This is the way toward beginning,
she has to reach through to a slim
sliver of ending. She has to reach
past the small burials, simple deaths,
and find her way through to another birth;
one more sun rising against the prairie sky.
The horizon lit far off in fire, and snow beckoning
for her footprints, shape of her heel,
silhouette of her shadow,
figure against a prairie league of snow.

WHEN THEO COVERED VINCENT'S COFFIN WITH SUNFLOWERS

North of Paris: July, 1890

He already knew his own death could feel it
making words inside his throat; it settled
like a node, a sketch of his own mortality.
For two days, Theo laid in bed with his brother.

The summer moon rose and fell over
the shadow of Vincent. And Theo wanted,
in the small moments of the end, to persuade
life into his brother, to cradle him in his arms.

He'd found him sitting up in bed.
The bullet, like a boy running through the fields
of Vincent's chest, like a crow searching out a place
to fall still, and Vincent lit a pipe and smiled.

Theo sat at the edge of the bed, took off his boots
and stretched out beside his brother, believed,
just for a small moment, Vincent would be all right.
He'd rise up in the morning, the wound fallen still

and quiet, and go into the fields, paint lovers
by a fence post, a crow with a blood-red beak
cawing overhead. Theo crossed his arms over his chest
and smiled as Vincent smoked his pipe.

When Theo covered Vincent's coffin
with sunflowers, he saw the sketch of his own death
moving inside him, the way syphilis traveled
through him like a bullet.

BE ALL MY SINS REMEMBERED, A POEM ON THE CONFESSIONAL

Like most Catholics, I am bound to the confessional. The booth is sometimes smaller than I've remembered and sometimes larger – I believe it fluctuates in direct relation to my sins. *Forgive me, Father, for I have sinned. It's been one week since my last confession.* I've held-back in the confessional. I don't know why. Sometimes I'm struck dumb, completely blank, and begin making sins up. I'll list off things I haven't done: dishonouring my mother, coveting my neighbour's belongings (sometimes I mention my neighbour's husband). When I'm really stuck and the booth seems to be shrinking, I begin listing off the deadly sins: pride, greed, lust, anger, gluttony, envy, sloth.

I often trail off uncertainly to be pulled back by, "Have you had any impure thoughts?" I shrug inside the now cramped quarters, "Sure," I say. Think if this were the least of my worries how blessed I'd be. My friend Alison tells me if I am a good person then I along with all the other good people get to go to Heaven. But you and I, we know that's not the case don't we? I often forget sins I mean to list: using the Lord's name in vain, behaving in an uncharitable manner, being unable or unwilling to turn the other cheek. It was the Catholic school system, which roped me in. It was the holy water on my fingers, it was the blood in my mouth, it was the flesh of God thin and narrow as the eye of a needle resting on my tongue.

It was the prophets and the blesseds. It was the saints. Their willingness to suffer: the beauty of the flames, the scorched flesh, the triumphant crack of their bones, the rip of their skin, and the way Saint Margaret stood over the dragon. She was triumphant and assured a direct and well lit path to Heaven. I lied, cheated, and stole. I falsified documents and took illegal narcotics, and I sold them. I drank too much on occasion and left my bestfriend in a brightly lit corridor because she couldn't handle angel dust. Although, I don't know many who can. When I was a young girl, I left a young boy in the Dawson Creek General Hospital emergency room due to alcohol poisoning, and I left without leaving my name or knowing if he'd live.

I skipped town without paying my rent. I told bill collectors I was dead, or someone else and too busy to talk to them because I was playing Nintendo. I parked in the handicap parking, drove not only without a valid driver's license, but also without insurance, and at the same time with, by the way, an unlicensed firearm in the vehicle – and a case of beer. I have had more than one warrant out for my arrest. There is no one here, but you and me. In the confessional, there is no one here, but you and me. So lean a little closer, and let me tell you – I was reckless. I believed, I could never satisfy my own hunger. Starving, I went to him and parted my stomach – this for pain and this last part for all the pleasure I wasn't supposed to have.

Shhh, I won't think about it. I'll choose what I'll remember, pick what I can contain, recognize what I can bear, and I'll chuck the rest of it. I don't know where it goes, but do I have enough time to beat it back, memories rising up, before they get a hold of me, and haul me under? I won't concentrate on the small details. Let's agree to leave one room locked and shuttered. And who keeps opening that door? Which one keeps opening the door? And I remember, from Catechism class, the sins crying out to Heaven for vengeance. I'm an arsonist and there is a waste land behind me; I can't help myself. Maybe I'm just fond of that crack of wood when the flame gets in there? I think, it reminds me of Saint Joan –

the snap of fire, burning oak, cedar and plywood, all of it up in flames. Behind me, I've left a waste land. I don't know how to stop saying, *I'm sorry.* Or how to cease from muttering, *Forgive me, for I have sinned.* I have left a trail of trash bins and rubbish heaps. I've left a waste land behind me. Flames flickering in the night, and rivers I can never cross for sweet, the smell of all my burning bridges. I am responsible for everything I've done, and it sings inside me. It is the motion of a cricket, at twilight that endless scratch, sing, scratch, sing. I want you to forgive me, and I want you to understand. There's a gothic grille, a laced window separating you and I. And I loop my fingers of both hands through the lattice – I want to be absolved. *Will you hear my confession?*

I did things I didn't want to do. Isn't that what sin is? It's cooperation; it's conforming; it's corroborating, concurring, and conceding. It's making concessions, and it is reconciling. And it seems to sit so close – I can't pull absolution away from cooperation and contrition seems connected to compromising. God's hand was a fist around my heart. I felt his breath against my back; his wrath at the edges of my mind. Everyone, but that one man, pronounced my loneliness. The seagulls followed me home, the ravens stood by my door, sat on the ledge of my window, and they wept and wept. *Forgive me, for I have sinned. O my God, I am heartily sorry for having offended Thee, and I detest all my sins because of Thy just punishments, but most of all because they offend Thee, my God, Who are all-good and deserving of all my love. I firmly resolve, with the help of Thy grace, to sin no more and to avoid the near occasions of sin.* I push my fingers through the wooden lace, which separates you from me. I lift my head up, my eyes to your eyes. I gave myself away, but only he matters. *Only he matters.* I will give myself to him. I will uncover myself in the meadow with winter still a chill in the air, and with the crocuses opening. I will stare at the heavens as he comes into me. I will say his name, warm breath, against his neck. I love him. I didn't think this would ever happen, and so sweet the taste of sin.

I knew a man. He was proud, arrogant, over-confident, over-bearing, vain, and filled with self-importance. I set aside his faults and watched how weakness sat twinned with strength. Do you see it? *Weakness twinned with strength?* Removal of one means removal of the other, and what pieces would any of us have left? To be proud is to be inflated as well as noble. His arrogance was some-how charming, and I held his sin in my hands. I have caught myself recently lathering this sin up as if I found it on Victoria Street in one of those over-priced shops which smell of Vanilla and Lavender. I am embarrassed, ashamed, when I hear myself making wild declarations of love – my mouth cherry-red lollipop-lickin' and, oh, so *so* proud.

I am greedy and want it all. I want it all. I want everything. The world is a smorgasbord; it is a reservoir; it is an endless league of pine beetles, carpenter ants, parasites, and Starbucks™. I want everything. I want the Mulberry bag for £350; I want the boxed-set of Metallica; I want a red dress from Shanghai; I want amazing tickets to Rilo Kiley. I want a new car, property, land, poplar trees, red roses in a pale pink vase; I want everything. I want him. I do. I want him to cross continents, to cross oceans to come to me because I have desire; I have greed, need, wants. I want him. I want him to love me; to pick me. I cringe as I hear the words whispering inside me, hidden between my shoulder blades, *all I want is everything.*

Lust is a virgin, and she is wearing all the wrong clothes and stumbling along the railway tracks looking for someone to love the blood out of her. Lust moves like wet cement underneath all our feet. Lust is the devil crawling out from underneath my bed. His eyes are such a pale blue they look like violets, his breath is soft and warm and smells of jasmine. He brings me lilacs, in September, in his trembling hands. And his hair is a field of sunflowers, his palms unmarked, and his flesh as soft and cool as peeled almonds. He tells me all the ways he has come to love me, and my sins pour from my hands and feet, a soft roar of blood. I can taste wood and nails, my tongue is wrapped in a crown of thorns, and I hang my head in shame.

There are things I've done – anger has moved underneath my skin – a serpent slithering through muscle, the rattler inside my mouth, the boa-constrictor inside my chest, and my voice escalating as if it would reach all the levels of Heaven, deafen the rings of hell, quell the insistent rush of rational thought which ebbs inside blood, slow to the call. Once I screamed and slammed the doors. Once anger moved through me until I pounded on my chest bone, beat myself, pulled my hair, and I awoke in the quiet of the morning, magpies in the air. Crows called me through their flight in the air, and bruises over my breasts, clumps of my long red hair along the stairwell – all the way down into the world. I descended as if my rage lifted me like wings into the arms of the Virgin.

I am haunted and sing him cantos from across an ocean. My desire moves past lust and reaches out to gluttony. I am ravenous. I am insatiable. I feel emaciated. I pull my hair from my head, my arms bruised. Gluttony has so little to do with food and so much to do with *appetite*. My fragility sings there is something, which will bring him to me. My arms are empty, my ribs are discoloured, and I search out bones beneath pink flesh. I will subsist on the Eucharist and the smallest amounts of food. I will finish nothing. An empty plate is *empty*. I want to be empty. Am I nothing, but this sin? Bruised raw, made ravenous by desire to touch the back of his neck with my mouth?

I pine for him, hunger, desire, want. Yes I do, yes I do, *yes I do*. I wish, yearn, sigh, and crave not to mention thirst, hunger, and hell, I even hanker after. I fancy, relish, itch and long. I long for him and *envy her*. I am the green-eyed monster. I resent her, begrudge her. I am filled up with jealousy and it tears down all my walls like heartburn in the chest, and I comb my long hair in the mornings and tell myself that I am good. I am good. I am good enough. Envy makes me vigilant, watchful, attentive, guarded, and defensive. Envy makes me imagine the worst. I feel, foreign thing moving beneath my skin, insecure and threatened. I am, pink, vulnerable. And in my dreams he tells me, coffee cup in his hands, all the ways he will never want me.

There is the uneasy mind. There is the apathy. The sloth-ful brain, filled with sorrow. Sorrow, deliberately and self-directed, to turn away from God. To step away because I feel his love is insufficient. I want to love him. There is one step. Then there is another step, he doesn't call (enough), he doesn't write (enough). I am filled with doubt and self-recrimination, and my mind worries its way in a circle of loneliness. Oh, such a mild step, but to find anguish in the steps, to find regret, to fall idle and listless, to lose God. To realize the absence and the insufficiency of my own love is to feel shame. To guard myself against my own doubts, to be vigilant, to move love and affection like a ship searching for safe harbour. To love, to worship – God.

I make mistakes as if mistakes are a valued commodity. I've made mistakes as if I was given a small number and an end date by which to fulfill them, and they clamber along behind me – sometimes screaming at a deafening roar, "I am not the same as sin." *Remember, Christian soul, that thou has this day, and every day of thy life: God to glorify, Jesus to imitate, The Angels and Saints to invoke, A soul to save, A body to mortify, Sins to expiate, Virtues to acquire, Hell to avoid, Heaven to gain, Eternity to prepare for, Time to profit by, Neighbours to edify, The world to despise, Devils to combat, Passions to subdue, Death perhaps to suffer, And Judgment to undergo.* Forgive me, Father, for I have sinned. I'm on bended knees, Father. Father … Father, *Father, please.*

THE RAISING OF LAZARUS

Saint Rémy: May, 1890

Only skull caps and Metallica can pull her from her rest.
Only guitars and amplifiers and lager can pull her
from her slumber. Only cigarettes and beer can wake her,
wake her, wake. Her dying is a tattoo of liquid,
a mark like Cain, a stain of crimson and blood,
and blood, and only her, her, her dying, wake. Wake.
Army boots and bags, lime-green toque, t-shirts,
and jeans, cigarettes, and beer at her wake, her wake,
at her wake. And my brother, her father, won't go
to such a wake. He sits by her body waiting for her,
waiting for her, waiting, wading through the water
of her death, and he is waiting, waiting for her to wake.

I WOULD GIVE HER SASKATCHEWAN

she writes, her mother was borne
between rosary and choir.
not orphaned, but left by choice
to the nuns. left to the skip of beads,
and hum of prayer. her mother was left
to the care of voices soaring to the saints,
blesseds, prophets, up to God distant and obscure.

she writes, the trail she turns to look to,
and the places she turns to find herself
are missing. missing is a place, where she
can fall to doorstep, ancestors she can lift
to her brow like holy water. missing
the lists of names and places. the well of blood
belonging to her, making her, forming her

in heritage. this, perhaps, only something
recognized when missing. the rest of us,
possibly, thinking heritage a tag word
in a museum or gallery and not something
to be born from. our own mothers,
for the most part, not borne of rosary or choir,
but rather of semen and lust, of a long list

of names running out behind like ragged
shoe-laces; able to rattle off the names of men
and women trailing behind like bookends
and grave-marks. blood from birth and death,
from virginity lost only to be reclaimed
with each girl child, who comes running out after,
breathless and pink. the circular motion

of our blessings and abusings so clearly
and starkly marked in the bone. cree, scottish
and irish running like fresh horses in our veins
and able to say, this is what we've come from,
better or worse, a marriage which cannot
be undone. she writes, a cultural identity
might fill her hands, and give her something to hold.

i would give her my drunken scottish grandmother
with her wild red hair, thick as a horse's mane,
and i would give her to saskatchewan,
even though it's scotland she'd want, but she needs
land of wheat, acre of canada because this is the land
she belongs to; its soil is in her veins. a wondrous
gift of blood and earth. i want her to stand inside

a small moment, on a train with a bottle
of good canadian whiskey or okanagan wine,
and a quarter loaf of bread and a jar
of mennonite pickles. she's been traveling through
the cariboo out from the shadow of the coast
    mountains,
winding through the fraser valley into the interior
    plateau.
the train'll stop in cache creek, savona, kamloops,

and she'll sleep through the desert and wake-up
in the prairies. when the train pulls into
saskatoon, it's winter, and it's snowing; she
doesn't know, like the rest of us, where she belongs.
but canada is flowing through her métis veins,
and when she looks down she sees her cupped
hands filled with mixed-blood and its dark, rich soil.

The bear tells me, *I was the only one,*
I was the one who'd take her and wanted her.
Not the others. The ginger shape of his beard
is illuminated from the campfire, and I wonder
if it wasn't the way he tilted his head
which reeled her toward him like a caught fish.

I remember the animals which came
calling before him. The way she loved the raven
and his wide wings, the black folds
as good as soil, enough to keep her planted,
and at the same time help her soar.
This, the reason she moved toward the bee,

the sweet honeycomb of his innocence,
the sting of his passion, but she left him
because of his Romeo and Juliet dime-store
rip-off, his boundless body dance of direction.
All she saw before her: endless kilometres
of pollen and syrup. When the salamander

came, she loved the shape of him sliding
through her fingers, the smell of lake-water
left tracing her mound of Venus. And after
the rubber boa had left her, she still marveled
at his streak of yellow and blunt nose.
But it was the bear, the ginger prickle of his beard

against her skin, and it was his eyes smoke-
coloured blue in the moonlight. It was his acre
of gentleness, his solid goodness as she moved
towards him, towards his warmth, spooned her body
next to his, felt his beard caress her forehead,
his spirit hibernate next to her soul.

& your name is awake in my mouth. & I think of you.
You're like a Neil Diamond song; you're dust on the road
to Meadow Lake being kicked up by fresh horses & tired
cowboy boots. You're white linen hanging on my grand-
ma's clothes line. & I have woken your name in my
mouth. & I think of you in all the small, measured beats
& my heart has woken your name in my mouth. You're
an oasis filled with lonely palm trees & coconut shells on
the ground. You're black & white film in a 1969 Pentax
camera. You're a Polar Bear in Paris. Your name is awake
in my mouth. & tomorrow when you rise from sleep;
when you shake yourself from Scottish sheets you will
know the sleeping consonants, the slumbering vowels of
my name in your mouth.

Yes. I say, yes to Bach and no to Beethoven.
Yes to Pearl Jam and no to Celine Dion,
but who could really compare the two, really?
I say, yes to hips and breasts and flesh
and knee high socks, and I say, no
to the barefooted, no to the zucchini eaters.
No, I say, no to zucchini and not just no
to those crazy enough to eat zucchini.
I also say, no to cilantro, but yes to the sound
of the word: cilantro.

                        Cilantro.

I say yes to the beautiful, dark crown of your head.
I say yes to pink. Yes to Electric Pink,
yes to Paradise Plum, yes to the frost of Ice Blue Pink
lipsticks. Yes to lavender and lime green underwear,
but no to wearing them together. Yes to underwire bras.
Yes to cotton, no to polyester. Yes to flannel pajamas
and bedding and no to percale. Yes to kilims and sumaks
and no to wall-to-wall carpets. Yes to espresso
and French press and no to cone and flat bottomed
    filters.

Yes. I say, yes to God the Father, the Son,
and the Holy Spirit, and no, I say, no
to the inherent loneliness of atheism.
I say, yes to freckles and bruises against
alabaster skin and no to the burnt almond,
buttery blonde, Toast of New York
(Revlon lipstick'd) had too many Mai Tais,
light my cigarette bitch who looks like a long,
drink of (what was said in that Tarantino film?)
cocksucker. Yeah, that was it: *cocksucker*.
I say, yes to Tarantino and no to Oliver Stone.
Yes to Jack Gilbert and no to Paul Dugan.
Yes to Salma Hayek and no to Jennifer Lopez.
Yes to Saint Michael and no to the bringer of light.
I say, yes to piercing the eyebrow and no to piercing
the tongue. Yes to popcorn and no to chips.
Yes to raspberry jam and no to marmalade.
Yes to you and no to every other man because
I want   I want   you, I want.

Yes. I say, yes to pale, but no to chalky.
I say, yes to cats and no to dogs. I say,
yes to God, yes to the Holy Church of Rome,
yes to the Fourteen Holy Helpers, yes
to the blesseds, yes to the incorruptible,
yes to the saints, the arch angels, seraphims,
and I say, yes to body, yes to affection, passion
and desire. I say, yes to sex and no to chastity.
Yes to the Eucharist, yes to the flesh
and the blood of God inside my mouth.
I say, yes to limbs parted. Yes to the building
of my body from your rib. Do you hear me?
I was made from your rib, and can't you feel
the way I finish you, the way I count
and stroke your ribs, kiss your flesh, pull you
apart with my teeth. The way I say,
yes to you. I say, yes and I am afraid,
I am afraid you will say, *No.*

MY VOICE

My voice is the screech, the howl of Lilith
as she moves through the garden.
My voice is the dandelion, the spot of yellow,
gracing your front lawn. My voice is the whine,
the break-neck spin of tires along Fortune Drive.
My voice, my voice, *my voice* is weeping.
My voice is the twang of Alison Krauss,
and the rough Birch bark cackle of Kris Delmhorst.
My voice is a CRF450 Honda,
and riding it is like wrestling a rhinoceros
in the grasslands of the Thompson River.

My voice is Muddy Waters' blues guitar.
My voice is Minnie Mouse when she's had too many
    Bloody Marys
and is standing on the table inhaling helium
from birthday balloons. My voice is drunk and out of
    control.
My voice is weeping.
My voice is the spire of the Space Needle,
the docks of Ballard, the waves of Vashon,
the Bainbridge Ferry moving past Little New York.
My voice is a broke down Volvo on the I-5.

My voice is weeping.
My voice is a tart, sour candy.
My voice is a strand of red hair being carried
off in the beak of a crow. My voice burns all bridges.
My voice is an accident waiting to happen.
My voice is an arsonist and has left a wasteland in its
    wake.

My voice is weeping.
My voice makes mistakes as if they're valued
    commodities.
My voice is a thief in broad daylight,
sunshine on the dark, punk crown of her head
and her bag from Value Village stuffed to bursting.
My voice renounces, it redeems, it massages, it desires.
My voice is the quilt made for my grandmother's wed-
    ding day.

My voice is weeping.
My voice is the door slamming.
It's the shadow against the sand, it's the bells
ringing on Sunday morning, it's beckoning.
My voice is beckons; it calls; it wants; it implores.
My voice is in love.
My voice is in love with you.
My voice is in love, and it's weeping.
My voice, *my voice* is weeping.

EPILOGUE

You. You are so reckless. You fall toward disaster
with your skull cap and DC shoes. I do not imagine
resurrection or redemption, but rather reverse.
The way back as if it could be as easy as moving

the gear shift into "r." As if by driving backwards he
could reach you before the car went into Jamieson
    Creek.
He wouldn't mind if he even got there so that he
had to wade into the water and retrieve you.

I'd like to hit rewind, so that he could come find you,
and fetch you back to the living. Do you know,
Van Gogh believed that after he died he would live
among the stars? That Juliet thought they ought to cut

Romeo into star-shaped light, and he'd make
the face of heaven so fine? But I would plant you
in a field of green. You're so reckless. You
court disaster with your crooked smile and flushed face.

The opening quotation is from Richard Van Camp's novel *The Lesser Blessed* (Douglas & McIntyre, 1996).

The title for "On the Revolutions of the Celestial Orbs" is a translation of Nicolaus Copernicus's 1543 *De Revolutionibus Orbium Coelestium* sometimes translated as *On the Revolutions of the Heavenly Spheres*.

The titles "Perfectly Still in the Wind" and "How He Carried Her Back Cradled in His Arms" are from Patrick Lane's "Winter 19" and "Winter 44" respectively, and both appear in his book *Winter* (Coteau, 1990).

The titles of the poems incorporating and using Vincent Van Gogh's paintings are primarily taken from the title of his works.

The prologue is for my brother, Kevin MacLeod; "On the Revolutions of the Celestial Orbs" was a ghost of a poem until I read it to David Houseman, in this way it is as much his poem as it is mine; "Perfectly Still in the Wind" was written for Rebecca Fredrickson; "The Small Burials" is for my mother, Mazie Ann Beeds; the epilogue is in memory of little Sarah Grace.

ACKNOWLEDGMENTS

Grateful acknowledgment is made to the editors of the following publications in which these poems first appeared some in earlier versions: *Clay Palm Review*: "A Small Demon in the Blood" and "I Would Give Her Saskatchewan"; *Event*: "She Married the Bear"; *CV2*: "Irit, Lot's Wife," "My Voice," and "Rebecca"; *The Fiddlehead*: "Still Life: Bottle, Lemons and Oranges"; *Green Stone Mountain Review*: "When Erin Fought Beside Joan of Arc"; *JAAM*: "The Way Katy Lost God"; *The Prairie Journal*: "The Serpent"; *Room*: "Field of Wheat with Crows" and "The Small Burials"; *subTerrain*: "Be All My Sins Remembered, A Poem on the Confessional."

"Essence" and "Then She'd Know" were published in the chapbook *The Shapes of Orion*, edited by Brad Cran (Smoking Lung Press, 2000).

The poem "On the Revolutions of the Celestial Orbs" was adapted into a play while I worked on a Master's degree at the University of Edinburgh.

My thanks to the Canada Council for the Arts and the BC Arts Council for grants that supported me during the writing of this book as well I am grateful to the University of Alberta for the Patrick Folinsbee and the William Rea scholarships.

Thanks to my friends, family, classmates, and teachers for their generosity and humor. In particular, thanks to Trisia Eddy, Mary Finlay-Doney, Katy E. Ellis, David Houseman, Peter Murphy, Jennifer Rensch, Medha Samarasinghe, and special thanks, and with immense gratitude, to my mother Mazie Ann Beeds and my brother Kevin MacLeod.

Heather Simeney MacLeod has three previous collections of poetry: *My Flesh the Sound of Rain*, *The Burden of Snow*, and the newly released *Intermission*. Her poetry, fiction, nonfiction, and reviews have appeared in many journals and magazines. Her creative nonfiction piece, "How to Discover the Various Uses of Things," was a finalist in the 2011 CBC Literary Awards. She is currently a PhD candidate in the Department of English and Film Studies at the University of Alberta.